D1384453

THE BOSTON
TEA PARTY

Essential Events

THE BOSTON
TEA PARTY

BY IDA WALKER

Content Consultant
Michelle LeBlanc
Education Director
Old South Meeting House
Boston, Massachusetts

ABDO
Publishing Company

CREDITS

Published by ABDO Publishing Company, 8000 West 78th Street, Edina, Minnesota 55439. Copyright © 2008 by Abdo Consulting Group, Inc. International copyrights reserved in all countries. No part of this book may be reproduced in any form without written permission from the publisher. The Essential Library™ is a trademark and logo of ABDO Publishing Company.

Printed in the United States.

Editor: Paula Lewis
Cover Design: Becky Daum
Interior Design: Lindaanne Donohoe

Library of Congress Cataloging-in-Publication Data
Walker, Ida
  The Boston Tea Party / Ida Walker.
     p. cm.—(Essential events)
Includes bibliographical references and index.
  ISBN 978-1-59928-849-9
1. Boston Tea Party, 1773—Juvenile literature. I. Title.

E215.7.W35 2008
  973.3'115—dc22

                                        2007012150

TABLE OF CONTENTS

An artist's depiction of British tea being destroyed in Boston Harbor

THE MOST FAMOUS TEA PARTY IN HISTORY

On December 16, 1773, as many as 5,000 people crowded into Boston's Old South Meeting House and onto the nearby streets. The colonists were fed up with how they were being treated by the British government—which included Thomas

Hutchinson, the governor of the Massachusetts colony. For the past few years, the British government had placed taxes on many items necessary to the colonies.

While taxes had been repealed on some items, the British stubbornly refused to lift the tax on tea—the favorite beverage of many colonists. Not only did the British refuse to do away with the tea tax, they made it easier—and less expensive—for Britain's East India Company to sell their tea to the colonies. This meant that the East India Company could charge less and sell more tea than the colonial merchants.

This was a constant reminder of Britain's right to tax the colonies without its representation in the British government. Frustrated and angry, a group of Boston colonists decided to protest.

Samuel Adams led the meeting at the Old South Meeting House. The group discussed how to prevent three ships (the *Dartmouth,* the *Beaver,* and the *Eleanor*) carrying a shipment of tea from the East India Company from unloading their cargo in Boston. If that was not

Not Just One Tea Party

The most famous tea party in history was not the only one held in Boston to protest British tax policies. A second tea party was held on March 7, 1774. This protest was much smaller, with only 16 chests of tea from Davison, Newman & Co. dumped into the harbor.

possible, they wanted to prevent British authorities from collecting the duty on the ships' contents.

The Patriots urged Francis Rotch (representing the *Dartmouth*) to meet with Hutchinson at his summer residence in Milton, Massachusetts. Rotch was to ask the governor to issue a pass allowing the *Dartmouth* to leave the harbor without unloading the tea. Rotch was to return to the Old South Meeting House by three o'clock that afternoon to inform the Patriots of the governor's reply.

Those assembled in the meeting house were waiting, with varying degrees of patience, for Rotch's return and the governor's response. The reply to their demands would determine what action would follow. Finally, Rotch returned around six o'clock. Hutchinson would not issue a pass for the *Dartmouth* to leave the harbor—and Rotch was unwilling to move his ship without permission.

On hearing the news, the grumbling grew louder and became shouts and calls for colonists to take immediate action. "Let every man do his duty and be true to his country" echoed among the crowd.[1] The meeting ended, and some of the men quickly left to prepare for the next part of their plan.

Later that evening, Mohawk Indians, or so it seemed, carried tomahawks and clubs as they quietly walked down the street toward Griffin's Wharf at Boston Harbor. However, these "Mohawks" were actually colonists. They had painted their hands and faces with coal dust as a disguise to hide their true identities, even from each other.

As they neared the harbor, the men could see the *Dartmouth,* the *Beaver,* and the *Eleanor* sitting in Boston Harbor. The men divided up into three groups of about 50 men each, one group for each ship. With yells, whoops, and other battle cries, the men stormed the ships. Tomahawks were raised and brought down in crushing blows onto the tea chests. Each chest was broken so that the saltwater would do as much damage as possible when it mingled with the tea dumped in the harbor.

It did not take long for a crowd to gather on the dock. Colonists had followed the disguised men down the streets of Boston. Some were content to stand and watch such an unusual—and dangerous—event. Others cheered and clapped in support. Then there were those who wanted to rescue some of the tea. As the tea chests were broken into, some of the crowd rushed aboard the ships to gather up as much tea as possible before it could be thrown into the ocean. Those who were caught stealing tea were forcibly removed from the ship. George Hewes was one of the disguised participants. He reported that an elderly man caught taking tea was allowed to escape, but not before his hat and wig were removed and tossed into the harbor.

George Hewes: An Eyewitness

One of the most complete accounts of what happened during the Boston Tea Party was provided by George Robert Twelves Hewes. A shoemaker, Hewes was an eyewitness to more than one event in the birth of a new nation.

In 1768, Hewes became involved in the movement toward an independent country when a British soldier refused to pay him for a pair of shoes he had ordered. He protested against the heavy-handed methods British soldiers used to control the people of Boston. He also provided an eyewitness account of the Boston Massacre.

Hewes could never compete with the larger Massachusetts' shoemakers, and his participation in rebellious activities doomed his business. He was unable to pay his debts and was sent to debtor's prison in September 1770. If British authorities thought a prison stay would soften Hewes's Patriot leanings, they were wrong. He participated in the Boston Tea Party and served as a soldier during the War for Independence.

Hewes described what happened to Captain O'Connor, who had boarded one of the ships to collect tea:

> ... *when he supposed he was not noticed, filled his pockets, and also the lining of his coat. ... We were ordered to take him into custody, and just as he was stepping from the vessel, I seized him by the skirt of his coat, and in attempting to pull him back, I tore it off; but ... he made his escape. He had, however, to run ... through the crowd upon the wharf ... each one, as he passed, giving him a kick or stroke.* [2]

"It does not require a majority to prevail, but rather an irate, tireless minority keen to set brush fires in people's minds."[3]

—Samuel Adams

For three hours, the disguised men used their tomahawks and clubs to break open the tea chests and dump the contents into Boston Harbor. The action caught the attention of the British. While the tea was being dumped into Boston Harbor, armed British ships surrounded them and watched the action. However, they never tried to stop the colonists.

Once the tea was dumped into the harbor, the disguised men quickly left the ships. According to Hewes, except for those in charge, none of the individuals responsible for destroying the tea said a word. None of the participants made any effort to discover who else had been involved in the operation.

Such secrecy also meant that should someone be identified and questioned, he would be unable to name other participants. Anyone found guilty of being part of the incident could be imprisoned or sentenced to death. Their secrecy was effective. Only one person was sentenced for participating in the Boston Tea Party.

The light of the following morning showed that there was still more work to do in order to accomplish the goal of complete tea destruction. Early morning visitors to Boston Harbor found a great deal of tea was still floating on the water's surface. This time, however, it was not disguised men who took action. Ordinary citizens in small boats rowed over to the tea and, using their oars, beat at the tea until it sank, making it impossible for others to collect it for home use.

Actions such as the Boston Tea Party put the British government and its representatives in America on notice. Colonists were not willing to remain under a policy of taxation without representation. The policies were intolerable—and they would not go unchallenged.

Colonists disguised as Mohawk Indians dumping tea into the Boston Harbor, 1773

*Both Britain and France claimed the land between
the Appalachian Mountains and the Mississippi River.*

CHALLENGING THE COLONIES

he path to the 1773 Boston Tea Party
began with a power struggle between
Britain and France, the two superpowers of the
eighteenth century. Each country wanted to
dominate the New World. This mutual desire
resulted in a struggle over land in America.

The French and Indian War

By 1754, it was clear that the French and the British would do battle. The area in question was called the Ohio Country, although its territory extended far beyond what is known as the state of Ohio today. Both Britain and France claimed the land between the Appalachian Mountains and the Mississippi River and from the Great Lakes to the Gulf of Mexico. Both powers built trading posts and forts to establish their claims to the land. The French and Indian War would eventually settle the question of which country controlled the emerging nation.

Individuals living in British colonies were concerned about how their lives would change should France gain control. Many colonists had come in search of religious freedom. The British colonists were mostly Protestant. France was Roman Catholic, and the prospect of Roman Catholic rule threatened many of the British colonists.

The New World

When explorers and then colonists came to North America, they referred to it as the New World. Europe became known as the Old World. Those labels are accurate only to a point.

Europeans were not the first people in North America. The Europeans interacted with the First Nations people who were native to the area that is now Canada. In America, newcomers encountered the American Indians, who played important roles in the survival of the country's newest residents. To the First Nations people and the American Indians, this "New" World was not so new.

Major conflict in the French and Indian War began in 1754. Despite attempts by the British to negotiate, the French refused to leave their forts peacefully. Twenty-two-year-old Major George Washington and colonial troops from Virginia were sent to the French camp at Fort Duquesne (present-day Pittsburgh, Pennsylvania). When they encountered the French, a brief battle occurred in which one French officer was killed. Washington retreated and established Fort Necessity, a British fort, nearby. French soldiers easily attacked the fort; Washington was forced to surrender.

One and Only Defeat

Washington's defeat at Fort Necessity was the only time he surrendered in his military career.

The war appeared to be going in favor of the French—until the conflict spilled over to Europe. In May 1756, Britain declared war on France; the Seven Years' War began in Europe.

Both countries were now split between the continuing conflict in the colonies and a growing war in Europe. This two-edged war proved to be France's downfall. In 1756, Secretary of State William Pitt took over the British leadership of the war. The British efforts in the French and Indian

War became more organized—and successful. France, however, concentrated on the conflict in Europe, the battles in the colonies became much less important.

Fighting in North America continued until 1760, when the French surrendered Montreal, and Canada fell to Britain. The French and Indian War did not officially end until the Treaty of Paris was signed on February 10, 1763. The treaty also ended the Seven Years' War in Europe. France lost its presence in the North American territory east of the Mississippi River, except for two small islands in the Caribbean. Spain was given Louisiana to make up for losing Florida to Britain. Great Britain was now the dominant force in North America.

Under the Treaty of Paris, France had to agree not to build any military sites in India. This opened the door for Britain to dominate India as well.

Britain achieved what it had set out to do—control North America. Control of India was a bonus.

Paying the Bill

The British now had control over North America, but they also had a problem—a big one. The wars in North America and Europe had been very expensive. The British treasury was dangerously low. Parliament needed to find a way to increase the amount of money coming into the government.

There was no way around it; Britain had to raise taxes. But, Parliament did not want to increase taxes on its citizens. It seemed obvious to many that the colonies, on whose behalf Britain claimed the wars had been fought, should help pay the expense. In 1764, Parliament passed the Sugar Act, the first new tax designed to pay off the expense of war. The act was a revision of the Sugar and Molasses Act, which had been passed in 1733. The earlier act placed a tax on molasses imported from the West Indies. This made products imported from England less expensive than those imported from the West Indies. The law had largely been ignored by the colonists who found bribing local officials and smuggling to be effective ways around the requirements.

The Sugar Act of 1764 actually lowered the tax the earlier act had placed on molasses. However, it also increased the number of items

Representation, Not Independence

Initially, the colonies were not interested in gaining independence from the British. They did not see the need to become a new country. The Patriots sought representation. If the British government was going to tax them, they felt they had the right to have a say in how that money was used. As British citizens, the Patriots believed they had the right to provide input on how they should be taxed. If the colonies had representation in British Parliament, independence was not needed.

that were taxed. Wine, cloth, and coffee were just some of the items that fell under the Sugar Act. The new act also contained provisions regarding the enforcement of the law. Officials were given the authority to seize smugglers' goods without first getting approval from a court. This made it difficult for the colonists to work around the law.

Samuel Adams tried to build up opposition to the Sugar Act, but his success was limited. Most colonists agreed that the Sugar Act was unfair, but they saw no way to get Parliament to reverse its decision. The colonies had no representatives in Parliament. Many colonists resented this. Cries of "no taxation without representation" became more frequent, and the Stamp Act would make these protests even louder.

Forgotten Participants

As Britain and France battled over the control of the colonies, the American Indians were ignored. Neither the British nor the French were concerned with the American Indians' claims that the land was rightfully theirs. The American Indians joined in the conflict that raged on their lands. Most fought with the French, but the Iroquois fought alongside the British.

The Stamp Act of 1765

Britain had another problem in addition to paying for the French and Indian War and the Seven Years' War. Running the colonies was expensive. The British looked for a way to make the colonists pay for some of those expenses. In 1765, Parliament passed the Quartering Act. This act required the colonies to be responsible for providing housing for British soldiers.

Parliament also passed the Stamp Act, which taxed every piece of printed paper. This required that all legal documents, permits, contracts, newspapers, pamphlets, and even playing cards carry an official embossed tax stamp or seal.

This pushed the colonists to their limits. The Stamp Act was to go into

Taking a Stand

Prior to becoming a political figure, Patrick Henry had failed as both a shopkeeper and a farmer. He turned to law, which led him to the Virginia House of Burgesses.

On May 30, 1765, Henry stood on the floor of Virginia's legislative body. He proposed a series of resolutions to be presented to King George III and Parliament. This was the newly elected Henry's first speech to the House of Burgess.

He started his speech by mentioning leaders who had been assassinated. Assuming Henry was suggesting King George III be murdered, cries of "Treason!" interrupted his speech. But, Henry continued by saying, "George the Third may profit by their example. If this be treason, make the most of it."[1]

With this speech, Henry took his first step into history. He was not afraid to speak his mind.

Henry spent almost all of the next 30 years in public office. He was a member of the Virginia Committee of Correspondence and the First Continental Congress. He led the Virginia troops as their commander-in-chief and served multiple terms as Virginia's governor.

Henry also was an important leader of the American Revolution. He believed in an individual's liberties. After the American Revolution, he worked toward the adoption of the Bill of Rights.

effect in November, and most colonists said they would not pay. When tax collectors were threatened with violence by the newly formed Sons of Liberty, many refused to enforce the tax and resigned. The seeds of resistance planted by Samuel Adams against the Sugar Act began to grow.

The Stamp Act united the most powerful members of the colonies. Lawyers, clergy, and businessmen worked together to oppose the Stamp Act. Colonial legislatures took up the matter. In May, Patrick Henry stood on the floor of the Virginia House of Burgesses and presented four resolutions stating opposition to the Stamp Act. A fifth resolution stated that only the colony had the right to tax its residents. Each of the five resolutions passed. However, a re-vote was taken the following day (in Henry's absence). The approval of the fifth resolution was removed before the document was sent to Parliament.

Stamp Act Congress

In June of 1765, representatives from the Massachusetts colony sent notices to all of the other colonies. The colonies were encouraged to formally oppose the Stamp Act and to meet to discuss their options. Most agreed, and all but four colonies were represented at the first Stamp Act Congress held in New York City in October.

Representatives passed the declaration of 13 rights and grievances written by John Dickinson from Pennsylvania. The declaration stated that American colonists were equal to British citizens in all ways. It also stated that Parliament could not tax the colonies unless they had representation in Parliament. Those assembled also vowed not to import British goods.

The Stamp Act became effective on November 1, 1765. As that date approached, violence against those who would enforce the act increased. In New York City, riots broke out. Word of the violence and opposition reached Britain. The King and Parliament realized it would be useless to even try to enforce the provisions of the act. In March 1766, the Stamp Act was repealed.

The King and Parliament may have thought all issues were now resolved. Soon though, they would find they were mistaken.

Stamp Act protestors burning stamps in New York City

King George III

FANNING THE FLAMES

olonists took pride in their victory over the Stamp Act. However, if they thought King George III and Parliament were ready to give in on the issue of colonial representation in Parliament, they were wrong. The British government was far from ready to surrender their right to rule.

The British government reasserted its dominance over the colonies the day the Stamp Act was repealed. On March 18, 1766, Parliament passed the Declaratory Act. The colonists did not immediately recognize the importance of the Declaratory Act. According to this act, Parliament had the right to make any laws that it wanted, and the colonists could do nothing about it. Once again, Parliament made a point of reminding the colonies that they were subordinate to, and dependent upon, the British government.

The colonists responded by not taking the act seriously. To many of the colonists, the act was simply an attempt by the British government to save face. After all, the colonists had forced Parliament and King George III to repeal the Stamp Act in 1766.

The British government had won some and lost some in its attempts to get the colonists to pay, or at least help pay, their own way. In 1767, the British tried again, this time with the help of Charles Townshend.

King George III

Britain's King George III was a powerful monarch. Of German ancestry, he was born and educated in England. In 1760, at the age of 22, he was crowned king.

In 1810, King George III became disabled by an illness that caused blindness and senility. These periods of insanity eventually caused political problems. His son Prince George acted as regent from 1811 until the death of King George III in 1820.

THE TOWNSHEND ACTS

Charles Townshend was skilled in politics. He was concerned with what he saw happening in England after Parliament repealed the Stamp Act. By 1767, rising tax rates were setting off riots in England. Townshend saw tax reform as a way to further his political career.

As the treasurer in the British cabinet, Townshend was responsible for economic and financial matters. He understood how the expenses of the French and Indian War and the continued support of the colonies negatively affected Britain. If the government could not earn enough money from the colonies to pay their bills, it would be necessary to raise taxes on people living in Britain. The British people let their displeasure be known.

Townshend was certain that there was a solution to what he saw as an unfair practice. Townshend's solution became known as the Townshend Acts. These acts imposed new taxes on the colonies.

In 1767, Parliament passed the individual laws that made up the Townshend Acts:

❖ The New York Restraining Act required colonial legislatures to provide British soldiers stationed in the colonies with shelter, food, and supplies.

❖ The Revenue Act was based on Townshend's concept of taxing only products produced outside of the colonies. Paint, tea, coffee, cocoa, glass, and lead were among the colonies' imported items, with tea being the most imported product. Those items would be taxed, and the money would go toward paying the salaries of colonial governors, judges, and other officials appointed by the British government.

❖ The Board of Customs Act created customs commissioners in Boston. They would collect the taxes required by the Revenue Act. The Board of Customs Act also created admiralty courts in Boston, Philadelphia, and Charleston. Admiralty courts had a judge, but no jury. The judge received a portion of any fines that were paid. The judge could also authorize the use of special search warrants.

Charles Townshend

Charles Townshend was charming. He had a wonderful sense of humor, was a good speaker, and was very intelligent. So, why did he make such poor decisions?

According to historians, Townshend could not anticipate the long-term effects of his policies. His every move seemed to be aimed at increasing his visibility in order to achieve a higher office. His political ambitions had negative effects on his relationships with others.

Shortly after the Townshend Acts were passed, Townshend died. The acts strained the relationship between Britain and the colonies.

Merchant Agreement

On August 1, 1768, the Boston merchants agreed to the following in protest of the Townshend Acts:

That we will not send or import from Great Britain this fall ... any other goods than what are already ordered. ...

That we will not send for or import any kind of goods or merchandise from Great Britain ... from January 1, 1769, to January 1, 1770, except salt, coals, fish-hooks and lines, hemp, duck, bar lead and shot, wool-cards, and card-wire.

That we will not purchase ... any kind of goods imported from Great Britain from January 1, 1769, to January 1, 1770. That we will not import ... or Purchase from any Who shall import from any other colony in America, from January 1, 1769, to January 1, 1770, any tea, glass, paper, or other goods commonly imported from Great Britain.

That we will not, from and after January 1, 1769, import into the province any tea, paper, glass, or painters' colours, until the Acts imposing duties on these articles have been repealed.[1]

THE COLONISTS RESPOND

The colonists continued to be taxed by the British government without representation in Parliament. The colonists' opposition to this practice increased. The Townshend Acts added to the colonial discontent.

For the colonists, the issue was self-government. To the extent it was allowed, self-government was important to the colonists. To the colonists, self-rule was a natural human right.

Townshend's arguments about taxes did not fool the colonists. It was obvious who would benefit from the Revenue Act. In Britain, taxes would decrease (or at least not increase as quickly). Meanwhile, the colonists' taxes would increase. The real issue was not whether goods were imported or produced in the colonies. Many colonists opposed taxation in general, particularly when they had little or no say in how they were being governed. The colonists protested again.

Determined to protest the Townshend Acts, particularly the Revenue Act, the colonists once again turned to nonimportation agreements. This meant the colonists refused to import or use the items that were being taxed. The method had proved effective before. The pressure placed on the British government led to the repeal of the Stamp Act.

THE POWER OF WORDS

There was something different about the colonial protests of the Townshend Acts. When the Stamp Act was passed by Parliament, many colonists responded with violence. This time, colonists turned to words as a form of protest.

On December 2, 1767, the first of John Dickinson's 14 "Letters from a Farmer in Pennsylvania to the Inhabitants of the British Colonies" was published in *The Boston Chronicle*. He called the Townshend Acts illegal and the suspension of the New York Assembly an attack on colonial freedom. In pamphlet form, the letters spread throughout many of the colonies. In February of 1768, Samuel Adams, with the approval of the Massachusetts House of Representatives, wrote the Massachusetts Circular Letter. Adams called for the colonies to unite and resist the British government. Many of the colonies followed with their own letters calling for change.

So far, disagreement had been mostly a war of words. But, the threat of violence was never far below the surface. In 1767, the British government revised the Quartering Act. Now, Americans had to let British soldiers live in their homes. Soldiers started arriving the following year. Sometimes, colonists threw insults and rocks at the soldiers. Though the situation was tense, serious violence was avoided. That would change.

THE BOSTON MASSACRE

Many Boston residents were unhappy to see British soldiers patrolling their streets in 1768. At first, residents kept their anger in check, and there was no violence. The longer the troops remained in the city, the angrier the colonists became. Groups of colonists often taunted the soldiers, throwing rocks, sticks, and angry words at the troops. Tensions grew and erupted in a riot on March 5, 1770.

That evening, a small group of colonists and soldiers exchanged insults. Before long, more than words flew between the citizens and the soldiers. The two groups began to fight. When the soldiers were forced back into their barracks, they may have thought this latest conflict was over. Instead, it had only begun.

Church bells began ringing in alarm. About 50 of Boston's citizens ran into the streets to see what was wrong. Suddenly, a young boy, with blood dripping down his face, ran down the street toward the crowd. He claimed that a British soldier had beaten him. The crowd hunted down and attacked the soldier. More British soldiers arrived. When colonists continued to pelt the troops, a soldier fired into the crowd, killing Crispus Attucks. Shots came from other soldiers. Two more men were killed, eight others were wounded,

The First Fatality

Crispus Attucks was born in 1723. His father, Prince, had lived in Africa but was brought to New England as a slave.

Attucks worked with his father on a farm. His family was treated kindly, but Attucks wanted his freedom. So his master sold him. His new master allowed him more freedom, but it was not enough. Attucks escaped on a whaling boat and became a sailor.

In 1770, Attucks arrived in Boston. On March 5, 1770, townspeople heard bells ringing and ran out to see what was going on. Attucks led a small group to the town square. He then gathered a group of colonists and challenged the British to fight without guns. Someone yelled, "Fire!" and a British soldier shot and killed Attucks. This is considered to be the first death in the War for Independence.

and two died of their wounds. The riot became known as the Boston Massacre.

Townspeople demanded that the soldiers be removed from Boston, and that those responsible for the deaths be brought to trial on murder charges. Two colonists, future president John Adams and Josiah Quincy II, defended the soldiers. Seven soldiers were found not guilty of murder charges. Two were found guilty of manslaughter.

For colonists, 1770 was a turning point. In April, their boycott of British goods led to the repeal of the Townshend Revenue Act, except for the tax on tea. The British government removed troops from the city after the Boston Massacre. The first blood had been shed in the War for Independence. Patriots, including the Sons of Liberty, looked toward the future.

British soldiers firing into the crowd in the Boston Massacre, 1770

*Colonial Patriots and British troops skirmish
at the site of the New York Liberty Pole.*

The Sons (and Daughters) of Liberty

rumbling among many colonists
increased with each passing day under
Parliament's rule. Parliament's refusal to
end the tax on tea renewed the Sons of Liberty's sense of
injustice that had been born with the Stamp Act of 1765.

THE SONS OF LIBERTY

Who were the Sons of Liberty? Some historians claim the first group formed in New York City in the fall of 1765. Most, however, pinpoint the beginning to a summer 1765 meeting of nine shopkeepers—The Loyal Nine—in Boston. In all likelihood, the groups formed about the same time. The purpose of both groups was to protest the newly passed Stamp Act. Eventually, each of the 13 colonies had a Sons of Liberty group.

In Boston, membership in The Loyal Nine quickly grew, so they changed their name. The name Sons of Liberty actually came from a member of Parliament. Isaac Barre was a supporter of the American colonies. During a debate in Parliament about the Stamp Act, he warned that the colonists, "these Sons of Liberty," would not stand for the tax.[1] The colonists, and the newly named Sons of Liberty, proved him right.

According to legend, the Boston group met under an elm tree near Hanover Square. The tree, which became known as the Liberty Tree, became an important symbol to the

The Liberty Tree

The original Liberty Tree was planted in the Massachusetts colony in 1646 and stood for almost 130 years. In August 1775, Loyalists cut down the symbol of freedom, leaving only a stump—the Liberty Stump.

Patriots. The Sons hung banners and lanterns in the tree as a form of protest. In 1765, the Sons of Liberty hung effigies of two tax collectors from the tree. Flags hanging on a pole near the tree signaled the Sons were to meet.

In New York City, the Sons of Liberty met under a Liberty Pole. As Sons of Liberty groups formed in all of the colonies, a Liberty Pole or Liberty Tree indicated a meeting place. Whether a tree or a pole, each was a symbol of the fight for freedom.

MEMBERSHIP

Speaking and writing against the British government and its policies were dangerous acts. Organizing and acting out against their policies was even more dangerous. For that reason, member-ship in the Sons of

Abigail Adams

Abigail Smith was born in 1744. Few women of her era received a formal education, and she was no exception. However, she was intelligent and read many books. This created a special bond with her future husband, John Adams.

Abigail Adams was not only married to a man who supported the Boston Tea Party, but she was also a woman who had her own strong opinions about the rights of women and the government.

Abigail Adams was ahead of her time. She believed in representation for women as well as men. She stated that if women were not listened to in the legislation of the laws, women should not feel obligated to obey those laws.

Twenty-four years after the Boston Tea Party, Abigail Adams's husband, John Adams, became the second president of the United States (1797–1801). Their son, John Quincy Adams, became president in 1825.

Liberty was secretive. The group tried to stay out of the public eye as much as possible. Membership was open to any male who could prove he was trustworthy and who had talents the organization could use.

"The tree of liberty must be refreshed from time to time with the blood of patriots and tyrants."[2]

—*Thomas Jefferson*

Early members of the Sons were workers and tradesmen, not members of the upper classes. Leaders of the Boston branch of the Sons of Liberty included legislator Samuel Adams and silversmith Paul Revere. Isaac Sears and Alexander McDougall led the New York Sons. Their reputation as self-made men earned them, and the Sons, the loyalty and support of much of New York City's working class. The Sons did not want to be openly associated with violence. When they needed a little more "muscle," they got others to step in.

The Sons Take Action

Most members of the Sons of Liberty did not favor the use of violence. However, two of the group's earliest actions included violent acts. On August 14, 1765, the Sons of Liberty showed their displeasure with the Stamp Act. Andrew Oliver was appointed to enforce the Stamp

Act in Massachusetts. The Sons of Liberty hung an effigy of Oliver in a tree. The tree also contained a boot, with a likeness of a devil climbing out of it. Clearly, the Sons associated Oliver with the evil they believed was represented by the Stamp Act. A large crowd quickly formed at the site. When British officials ordered the sheriff to take down the figures, he protested. No one could be certain what the crowd would do. The sheriff was right to be concerned. By the end of the night, protestors—not necessarily members of the Sons of Liberty—had stoned Oliver's house and beheaded and burned the effigy.

Extremist members of the Sons and their street fighters made their presence known in New York. In April 1765, a shipment of stamped papers arrived at the governor's home. Frightened at what the Sons might do, the acting royal governor locked himself inside Fort George. His concern proved wise when a large crowd showed up at the fort. They burned the governor's coach. The crowd continued to the home of Fort George's commander and vandalized his home.

Sons of Liberty penalize a person who looted tea after the Boston Tea Party by nailing his coat to a post.

Extremists might also tar and feather their opponents. Common targets included tax collectors. Despite these and other acts of violence, the Sons of Liberty considered their role to be that of organizers. They would organize protests against policies of Parliament, not commit acts of violence or attempt to disrupt the King's authority.

In protest of the Stamp Act, most colonies had passed nonimportation agreements. This meant that merchants were not to import items including tea, paper, and glass from Britain until Parliament removed the tax. Some merchants ignored the agreements—for a price. Those who did could expect a visit from the Sons of Liberty. New York City merchants caught violating these agreements had to make a public confession.

The Sons of Liberty also played an important role when the colonies formed the Committees of Correspondence. Through these committees, actions against Britain could be coordinated between the colonies. Newspapers were another way the Sons efficiently passed information to other colonies and individuals. Many of the Sons were printers and publishers, including Benjamin Edes and John Gill, early leaders of the Boston Sons of Liberty. Nearly every paper printed in the colonies carried accounts of the exploits of the Sons of Liberty. These reports helped the Sons increase their support among the population. It was not just men who supported the Sons of Liberty. Although society limited their political role, women were not about to be left out.

THE DAUGHTERS OF LIBERTY

Women became involved in the move toward independence long before the War for Independence began.

In the eighteenth century, society limited women's activities in politics. As husbands participated in political activities and pursued political careers, the women were not expected to be involved.

However, many women found ways to let their opinions be known. After passage of the Stamp Act and the formation of the Sons of Liberty, a group of women, most under the age of 40, formed the Daughters of Liberty.

The Daughters supported the boycott of British products. They organized spinning and weaving groups to make cloth that the colonies had formerly imported from Britain. Members also led the way in boycotting tea. Catnip, sage, and dried raspberry leaves were brewed as tea substitutes. Women in North Carolina signed a resolution

Saving the General's Life

Phoebe Fraunces, a young black girl whose father owned a tavern, saved General George Washington's life. Phoebe learned that Thomas Hickey, a bodyguard of Washington, planned to kill the general by poisoning his peas. Phoebe told her father and Washington. When Washington was served his food, one of his men fed the peas to the chickens. They ate the peas and died. Hickey was found guilty and sentenced to death.

supporting officials who pledged not to drink tea
or wear cloth produced in Britain. In Rhode Island,
women vowed to go without anything imported from
Britain. They even asked the men to do without alcohol
that came from Britain.

The names of many of the women who participated
in the Daughters of Liberty are unknown. However,
Sarah Bradlee Fulton has been called the "Mother of
the Boston Tea Party." Much of that evening's activities
were planned at her home. After dumping the tea,
many of the men returned to her home to change out
of their disguises.

Susan Livingston was the daughter of the New Jersey
governor. She prevented British soldiers from finding
military plans and lists of spies that were hidden in
her home.

Mercy Otis Warren wrote many letters that were
published in Boston-area newspapers. She also wrote
plays during a time when playwriting by anyone was
considered a less-than-desirable career. She even
dared to oppose the British government with some
of her playwriting. ⌐

Colonial woman spinning to avoid importing British cloth

Early colonial schoolroom

LIFE IN BOSTON

The early history of Boston was one of restrictions. Initially, only Puritans (Massachusetts's first British settlers) could live there. The leaders of the colony had little interest in changing things. Still, change did occur. By the mid-1700s, the Puritans had moved and

Boston and the rest of colonial America were ready for change.

One of the major factors leading to Boston's future as the origin of the American Revolution was its growth as a center of thinking. The first public school in America was established in Boston in 1635. Since its beginnings, the Boston Latin School encouraged differing viewpoints.

In 1636, Harvard College opened in nearby Cambridge. The school's purpose was to educate young men, many of whom went on to become Puritan ministers. Cambridge was also the site of the first printing press in the new colonies. During the days leading to the Revolution, as well as the conflict itself, the ability to use the printed word in order to spread information quickly was extremely valuable.

Boston's location was important to its growing economy. Not only an important trading site, Boston developed as a center for building ships. Before long, the port city of Boston had earned the reputation as the place for shipbuilding—not only in the colonies, but all

Boston Latin School and the Declaration of Independence

Founded April 23, 1635, Boston Latin School is the oldest public school in America. Boston Latin School can lay claim to helping plant the seeds of dissent in five of the signers of the Declaration of Independence: John Hancock, Samuel Adams, Benjamin Franklin, Robert Treat Paine, and William Hooper.

over the world. Its harbor also became the colonies' busiest seaport.

Eighteenth-century Boston

By the time of the Boston Tea Party, the city had existed for more than a century. The city and surrounding area had grown a great deal. With a population of approximately 16,000 people, Boston no longer had the restrictive atmosphere under which the early settlers lived. Harvard College and the availability of the printing press in America had opened the colony and its citizens to differing viewpoints. As the city's reputation as an intellectual center grew, so did its willingness to listen to the ideas and opinions of its citizens—even those who did not follow the popular opinion.

There was another important difference in Boston's citizens. Although immigrants to America were still arriving, most of the non-military people living in Boston at the time of the Boston Tea Party were born in America. For many, their parents also were born in America; for a few, even their grandparents were

Harvard Graduates

Harvard College (Harvard University today) was established 16 years after the Pilgrims landed in what became the Massachusetts Bay Colony. Since its founding in 1636, several U.S. presidents have earned honorary degrees from this prestigious university. George W. Bush graduated from Yale University and earned a master's degree from Harvard.

born in America. As a result, many colonists had no great emotional ties to England.

MAKING A LIVING

Shipping and trade played important parts in Boston's economy. Merchants such as John Hancock became wealthy by trading with Europe, Africa, and the West Indies. Cargos included the legal and the illegal, even slaves. Peter Faneuil, who made part of his fortune in the slave trade, became one of the most successful smugglers of the time.

Many colonists were skilled tradesmen. Professions such as shipbuilding and carpentry were considered to be prestigious in Boston. Silversmiths and furniture makers developed their crafts and worked hard to earn a good reputation throughout the colonies. The work of one silversmith, Paul Revere, is still admired in the twenty-first century.

Farming was another important occupation at the time of the Boston Tea Party. However, not all of those involved in agriculture lived on their farms. Because cities such as Boston were relatively small, some farmers chose to live in town, traveling to their farms as necessary. Of course, owning slaves also made it easier for farmers to live away from the farm.

In addition to growing crops of corn and other grains, farmers raised animals. The demand for wool grew during the eighteenth century. Sheep were raised and sheared of their wool. The fleece was sent to wool works built along the river for processing, where the fibers were spun into yarn to be made into clothing and household items.

Rivers were important to the growing logging industry. Trees were cut down in the surrounding woods and sent downriver for loading onto ships or to be used in other areas. Ironworks also developed along the rivers around Boston. Of course, fishermen took advantage of the

Elizabeth Murray

One woman who took full advantage of the opportunity to be involved in business was Elizabeth Murray. Born in Scotland in 1726, Elizabeth was orphaned as a young child. At 22, she settled in Boston. Her brother, James, sold two slaves Elizabeth owned to raise money. Using those funds and some credit he was able to obtain, James helped Elizabeth open a shop. A London company and a British fashion buyer helped Elizabeth keep her shop filled with goods that Americans could not get elsewhere.

As her skills as a businesswoman increased, she took on more responsibility in her shop and opened a boardinghouse. Not wanting to depend on others, Elizabeth went to London and learned how to keep the business's books and how to buy products for her store.

Elizabeth's independence extended beyond business. At the time, when women married, all of their property became their husband's. Elizabeth did not agree with this practice. Before her first two marriages, she created a prenuptial agreement to ensure that she was able to keep control of her property and finances.

bountiful fish in nearby waters.

Many women were involved in a variety of trades. Some, such as Elizabeth Murray, became successful businesswomen. At the time, women were limited to only a few professions, including dressmaking. Unlike the case in more recent history, men dominated the teaching profession.

EDUCATION

Eighteenth-century students were almost always boys. Girls were not sent to school. They were taught to read (and sometimes write) at home. It was thought to be more important for girls to learn to run a household. While some girls did receive music or voice lessons, most learned how to entertain, cook, and sew. Daughters of upper-class families learned how to handle cooks and nannies. It was not until 1789 that Massachusetts Lieutenant Governor Samuel Adams recommended passage of a law requiring education for girls.

Johnny Tremain

Written by Esther Forbes in 1943, *Johnny Tremain* gives readers insight into life in pre-Revolutionary America. Apprenticed to a silversmith, Johnny is forced to give up his silversmithing after an accident. He then works for a printer and newspaper publisher, carrying news to the colonists about the events of the day, including the Boston Massacre and the Boston Tea Party. During the course of the story, Johnny meets Patriots, including Paul Revere and Samuel Adams.

Johnny Tremain is one of the best-selling children's books of all time.

Boys from lower- or middle-class families (such as Paul Revere) might only attend a reading and writing school. Then, they were often apprenticed into a trade at the age of 11 or 12. Sons of middle- or upper-class families (such as John Hancock) might be able to continue their education. However, a lack of formal education did not keep men or women from playing important roles in their country's formation.

Rather than attend grammar school or college, many boys became apprentices. As an apprentice, a boy would work closely with an established master craftsman to learn a trade. Or, boys might be apprenticed to their fathers or other relatives to learn the family business. After a period of years, the apprentices were skilled enough to go out on their own or continue to work with their masters.

For some boys, apprenticeships were the best way to make a living. The wars leading to the Revolution had been difficult financially for families in the Boston area. Sending their sons to school was impossible. The sons had to help the family survive. These young men also helped a new nation to be born. ⌣

A young woodworker apprentice

Ladies and gentlemen having tea

The Party

Rather than be taxed on their beloved
British tea, colonists drank tea smuggled
from Holland. They also used local herbs and berries
to create new forms of tea. By boycotting British-taxed
tea, they intended to force Parliament to repeal the last
remaining tax of the Revenue Act.

Parliament was just as firm in its vow to keep the tax. However, the boycott by the colonies was having an effect, especially on the East India Tea Company. The sales of tea in the colonies dropped an amazing 70 percent in three years. This left the East India Company in serious trouble. It had little money and lots of unsold tea. To help the company avoid bankruptcy, Parliament passed the Tea Act in May of 1773.

The Tea Act was not just another attempt by Parliament to collect taxes from the colonists. The Tea Act not only allowed the East India Company to sell its tea directly to the colonies, but also to sell it at a price lower than that charged for the smuggled tea. Because they would still have to pay the tax, some colonists saw the Tea Act as a way to get the tax past the buyers.

The Tea Act also required that only certain colonial merchants be allowed to sell the tea—which limited fair competition. After all, perhaps the

John Hancock's Boycott

John Hancock had his own problems with tea. In 1768, his ship was seized by British customs officials. They claimed Hancock was smuggling. Though the charges were dropped, he ultimately faced hundreds of charges.

Hancock organized a boycott of tea from China, which was sold by the East India Company. Sales fell from 320,000 pounds (145,150 kg) to 520 pounds (236 kg). His boycott helped lead the company to near bankruptcy.

colonists would not mind paying the tax if the total cost of the tea was lower than that obtained illegally.

The colonists felt it was a matter of principle. The price was lower, but they would still be paying a tax—and still without representation in Parliament. It was not acceptable. With this move, the colonists had enough. It was time for action— time for a party.

PLANNING THE PARTY

The *Dartmouth* sailed into Boston Harbor on November 28, 1773. Samuel Adams and the Patriots were determined that the ship would not be allowed to unload its tea. Adams, members of the Sons of Liberty,

---

The *Gaspee* Incident

About 18 months prior to the Boston Tea Party, Rhode Island had its own uprising.

In 1764, Britain placed trade restrictions on the colonies to help pay for the French and Indian War and the costs of protecting the new territories. Britian made it illegal for the colonies to trade with anyone other than the British or merchants of the British West Indies.

Rhode Island depended on trade with many countries and chose to ignore the laws. Britain chose to enforce the laws. In 1772, William Dudingston, captain of the H.M.S. *Gaspee,* was assigned to patrol Rhode Island's bay to check boats for smuggled goods.

This angered Rhode Island's colonists, who felt the taxes and laws were unfair. On June 9, 1772, the *Gaspee* went after a small trading ship whose captain purposely led the *Gaspee* to shallow water where it ran aground. Approximately 60 colonists boarded the *Gaspee*. They defeated the crew, Dudingston surrendered his ship, and the *Gaspee* was set on fire.

Dudingston and his crew later identified many of the colonists, but no one was tried for participating in the attack.

and other Patriots patrolled the
streets of Boston to make certain
that the ship was not unloaded.
Massachusetts governor Thomas
Hutchinson (a British loyalist) was
just as determined that the tea would
be unloaded. His determination
increased when the *Beaver* and the
Eleanor sailed into port. They also
carried loads of cargo from the
East India Company.

Adams knew that there was a
limit to how long the tea-bearing
ships could remain in the harbor.
According to the Revenue Act, the
tea tax had to be paid within 20 days
of a ship's arrival. For the *Dartmouth*, that meant it had to
be collected no later than December 16. Adams and
Governor Hutchinson held their opposing positions.
Tensions were high among Boston colonists. Frequent
public meetings were held at Faneuil Hall (Boston's
town hall) and at the Old South Meeting House. Some
meetings attracted thousands of people. A resolution
was passed asking the merchants who had ordered the
tea to request that it be returned. These merchants were

Identifying the Indians

Several attempts have
been made to identify
the participants in the
Boston Tea Party. The
Boston chapter of the
Daughters of the Ameri-
can Revolution was able
to compile a list of 175
names, though much of
the information is based
on family histories, which
may not be accurate. It is
unlikely that it will ever be
known for certain who
participated in this important event.

loyal to the King and had been specifically selected to sell the tea. They refused to return the tea. Despite that, the *Dartmouth*'s owner, hoping to prevent possible violence, agreed to return to Britain. But to do so, he had to have permission from British officials. They refused and made plans to seize the ship for nonpayment of the tea tax.

While public meetings had been going on, Samuel Adams and Paul Revere were involved in behind-the-scenes planning. Representatives from the Sons of Liberty and other supporters met at the home of Sarah Bradlee Fulton to discuss their options should the governor and British authorities not back down. These Patriots were not going to let the tea be unloaded in their city. They would destroy the cargo if necessary.

The plan was risky. Anyone found to be associated with the act was sure to be punished, so it was important that participants be disguised. They decided to dress as Mohawk Indians. It would not be a perfect disguise, but it would do the trick. After the attack, they would quickly change their clothing and return to their homes.

A Dangerous Secret

Participating in the raid on the ships was a dangerous decision for the Patriots. If caught, they could have

been arrested and tried for treason.
Historians speculate that some of
the participants might have come
from wealthy families who would
not understand—or approve of—
participation in such an event.
Participants swore that they would
keep the plans secret and not tell
anyone the names of others who took
part. During the attack, many did not
acknowledge others, and silence was the rule. Most
never spoke of the raid. Those who did restricted their
comments to only close family members. It was a secret
most participants carried to their graves.

The Raid

Originally, the Boston Tea
Party was referred to as the
"Destruction of the Tea in
Boston Harbor."

The Protests Spread

Although participants' names might not have been
known, news of their action spread throughout the
colonies. An article in the December 20, 1763, edition
of the *Boston Gazette* describes the events of the evening:

> A number of brave & resolute men, determined to do all
> in their power to save their country from the ruin which
> their enemies had plotted, in less than four hours, emptied
> every chest of tea on board the three ships … amounting to

342 chests, into the sea!! without the least damage done to the ships or any other property. The ... owners are well pleas'd that their ships are thus clear'd; and the people are almost universally congratulating each other on this happy event. [1]

As news of the dumping of the tea traveled through the colonies, reports came that protests were being held elsewhere. In Lexington, the colonists burned all imported tea—not just British tea. Philadelphia and Charleston vowed not to allow ships carrying cargo from the East India Company to unload in their ports. The colonies were taking a stand.

The Sons of Liberty and their supporters had shown bravery in taking a stand on the issue of the tea tax. Most of the colonists favored the action. However, if the protestors thought dumping the tea would lead to dumping the tea tax and other restrictions, they were wrong. Still, they had much to be proud of.

Old South Meeting House

The site of the meeting was more than a meeting house. It was where the Puritans of Boston met for prayer. Built in 1729, the Old South Meeting House was Boston's largest building at the time of the Boston Tea Party.

After the Boston Tea Party, British soldiers took over the Old South Meeting House. The house of worship and birthplace of colonial protest was turned into a riding school. Pews became firewood, and soldiers put a bar in the balcony.

Interior of Old South Meeting House, the site of many tea tax protests

Samuel Adams, political leader and statesman

IMPORTANT PARTICIPANTS

Many people planned and carried out the Boston Tea Party. Samuel Adams, John Hancock, Paul Revere, and Thomas Hutchinson are just four of the many individuals whose lives were affected by the Boston Tea Party, the events that led up to it, and those that followed.

SAMUEL ADAMS

Samuel Adams was born in Boston on September 27, 1722. After graduation from Harvard, he began to study law. However, family pressure led him to taking a clerk position in a counting house. He left after a short while to try his hand at business. He had little luck, however, and lost most of his inheritance.

Adams then became a tax collector. He was not very good at that, either. His strength was in politics, especially political writing and strategy. His political essays appeared in the *Independent Advertiser*. Adams joined local political organizations and was elected to the Massachusetts legislature as a representative of Boston. He quickly rose in the ranks and soon had a position of leadership. British officials recognized Adams's potential, but he refused all appointments they offered him.

Adams was the driving force behind most protests over the Sugar Act and the Stamp Act. He knew Britain looked at the colonies as a source of income. His criticisms of Parliament policies were directly responsible for stirring the fires of colonial protest.

"All might be free if they valued freedom, and defended it as they should."[1]

—*Samuel Adams*

Adams's role in colonial politics did not end with the Boston Tea Party. He was a delegate to the First and Second Continental Congresses and became an outspoken supporter of independence for the colonies. Adams signed the Declaration of Independence. After the colonies won their independence from Britain, he worked to ensure that Massachusetts would pass the Constitution.

Adams served in the Massachusetts state senate and was an unsuccessful candidate for the U.S. House of Representatives. He served as lieutenant governor of Massachusetts from 1789 to 1793. From 1793 to 1794, he was the state's acting governor. On Governor John Hancock's death, Adams became governor. Samuel Adams retired from politics in 1797 and returned to his home in Boston. He died in 1803 at the age of 81, his place in history assured.

John Hancock

John Hancock is perhaps best known as the first signer of the Declaration of Independence. He was also the only person to sign it on July 4, 1776. However, his role in U.S. history goes much deeper.

Hancock was born January 12, 1737, in Braintree (now Quincy), Massachusetts. His uncle, a wealthy

Boston merchant, raised Hancock after his father died. Hancock graduated from Harvard and went to London to learn more about business.

In 1754, Hancock went to work for his uncle. Within ten years, he was managing the company. He became the wealthiest man in New England. He also became involved with protests against the Stamp Act. Customs collectors began to single him and his business out for extra scrutiny. When they charged him for the most minor violations, Hancock stood firm until the charges were dropped. His determination won him praise from the Patriot community.

> "The greatest ability in business is to get along with others and to influence their actions."[2]
>
> —John Hancock

Samuel Adams took Hancock under his wing, grooming him for politics. A successful merchant would be beneficial to the Patriot movement. Hancock's money, obtained both from legal trade and smuggling, helped finance much of the Boston area's resistance to the Stamp Act and other Parliament rulings.

Adams was a good teacher. In 1774, Hancock was chosen as the president of Massachusetts's Congress. In 1775, Hancock and Adams again joined forces.

Their speeches brought the pair to the attention of British officials.

Hancock was elected to the Second Continental Congress and eventually became president of the Congress. When delegates failed to elect Hancock commander-in-chief of the Continental Army, he resigned. He served as governor of Massachusetts for nine terms.

Hancock did not support the Constitution at first. It took the promise that he would receive the presidential nomination (if George Washington did not want it) to get him to support its approval.

Although Hancock did not achieve his two major goals—to become commander-in-chief and president— he did earn a place in U.S. history.

Paul Revere

Paul Revere was born in Boston in late December of 1734 or early January of 1735. After attending a local school, he was apprenticed to his father, a goldsmith. Revere earned a reputation as an excellent copper engraver and silversmith.

Revere was involved in colonial protests against British rulings almost from the beginning. Adams, with Revere, organized the Boston Tea Party. Revere

Paul Revere's engraving of the Boston Massacre, 1770

made many drawings and engravings that showed British oppression of the colonists. His most famous engraving depicts British troops firing their guns into a crowd of colonists during the Boston Massacre.

Most people remember Revere for his midnight ride. This famous ride was popularized (with adjustments to the facts) in the poem "Paul Revere's Ride" by Henry Wadsworth Longfellow. Although

The Regulars

It is unlikely that Paul Revere actually cried out "The British are coming" during his famous midnight ride. After all, the colonists were British as well. According to a guard at the house of Adams and Hancock in Lexington, Revere said, "The Regulars are coming."

Revere never made it to Concord on his April 18, 1775, ride, William Dawes and Samuel Prescott did. Between the three men, the warning got through, and British troops were turned away from Lexington and Concord.

The horse and rider system of carrying warnings and messages was likely Revere's most important contribution to the Revolution. The system was valuable in the war, and the warnings saved many lives.

During the American Revolution, Revere served in the Massachusetts militia. His military career was tarnished when a commanding officer accused Revere of disobeying orders and dismissed him. He later had a military trial and was cleared of the charges.

After the war, Revere returned to his previous work of making gold and silver items. He also became one of the colonies' leading bell casters. His skill and talent with metal work allowed Revere to achieve great financial success. In 1801, he started a copper and brassworks factory in Canton, Massachusetts that grew into Revere Copper and Brass, Inc.

Revere died on May 10, 1818. Bells that he had made rang, signaling his death.

Thomas Hutchinson

During the early days of colonial protest, few people were more disliked than Thomas Hutchinson, the governor of the Massachusetts colony.

Hutchinson was born in Boston on September 9, 1711. His father was a wealthy shipbuilder. Extremely intelligent, Hutchinson graduated from Harvard before he was 16 years old. After graduation, he worked in the counting room of his father's company. His intelligence was not limited to books. Through his own efforts, he soon owned a great deal of property.

As he progressed in business, Hutchinson became involved in Boston's politics. In 1737, he was selected to be a representative in the colony's legislature later that year. His views did not match those of the majority in the legislature and he left in 1740. He was, however, reelected in 1742.

When Hutchinson left the legislature in 1749, he was appointed to the Governor's Council. He was appointed lieutenant governor in 1758.

In 1761, as Chief Justice (or judge) of the Massachusetts province, Hutchinson issued search warrants that brought criticism and protests. Hutchinson did not personally support the Stamp Act. However, it was the law, and he was bound to enforce it.

Hutchinson became acting governor when Governor Francis Bernard resigned in 1769. When British troops attacked civilians during the 1770 Boston Massacre, Hutchinson gave in to the colonists' demands that the troops be removed.

In 1771, the British government named Hutchinson governor of the Massachusetts colony. His ability to govern the colony was limited as the British government maintained most of the control. Though Hutchinson had little real power, colonists saw him as being part of the British government. Their growing dissatisfaction, and the sometimes violent ways it was expressed, convinced the British government that a stronger presence was necessary. Hutchinson was replaced with a military governor. Hutchinson moved to England, where he died in London on June 3, 1780.

Royal Governor of Massachusetts Thomas Hutchinson

Benjamin Franklin

AFTER THE PARTY

Benjamin Franklin was in London working on a compromise between the colonists and Britain when the Boston Tea Party occurred. He was unaware of just how angry the Stamp Act had made the colonists. Franklin had no idea that the Patriots would act in such an extreme way.

In 1774, after word of the Boston Tea Party reached Britain, Parliament and the King were furious with the colonists. The Patriots had destroyed cargo, costing merchants a great deal of money. Worse than that, in the eyes of the British government, they had purposely broken the law. The colonists would be held accountable for their actions.

Franklin was ordered to appear before the Privy Council. As advisors to the King, the council members accused Franklin of treason against Britain. According to the Privy Council, Franklin gave the colonists information he had received from Governor Hutchinson to provoke riots and destroy the tea.

The Privy Council was right when it accused Franklin of passing along the Hutchinson letters. They had been given to him and he had passed them along to colleagues in Boston. Franklin asked that they remain private, but his request was ignored, and the letters were published.

Franklin silently listened to the words of abuse directed at him. Not once did he respond to their

Privy Council: Advisors to a King

King George III received advice from his Privy Council. This council was made up of advisors who gave confidential information and advice.

insults. His experience before the Privy Council convinced him that compromise was not possible. Shortly after, he returned to America and joined the call for change.

PUNISHING THE COLONY: THE INTOLERABLE ACTS

Parliament and the King were not going to settle for just giving Franklin a stern lecture. The colonists were going to have to pay for the destroyed tea, one way or the other. They had destroyed private property, and that was a crime.

In March 1774, Parliament passed the first of what became known as the Coercive Acts. To the colonists, these were the Intolerable Acts, laws they could not bear. The first act was the Boston Port Act, which went

---

The Chestertown Tea Party

Colonists used Committees of Correspondence to carry messages back and forth, but it sometimes took a long time for information to travel via horseback riders. The people of Chestertown, Maryland, did not learn about the Boston Tea Party until May of the following year—more than four months after the event.

Once the news reached Chestertown, the male residents held a town meeting. They passed a resolution calling on everyone in the community not to buy, sell, or drink tea until the British government repealed the tea tax.

These colonists also protested with a tea party of their own. In May of 1774, townspeople boarded a British ship that was carrying tea. Without disguises and in daylight, these citizens dumped the tea into the Chester River.

Each year, Chestertown celebrates with a reenactment of the event.

into effect in June. The Boston port was closed until the colony paid for the destroyed tea. Since most of Boston depended on the port in some way, its closing could cause a great deal of hardship.

In May 1774, two other acts went into effect. The Administration of Justice Act stated that British officials could not be tried in colonial courts. Any British official charged with a crime was sent to a different colony or returned to Britain to face trial.

The Massachusetts Government Act virtually ended self-government in the colony. The colony's charter was revoked. The British governor was given control of town meetings.

An Expensive Offer

Franklin not only urged Massachusetts to pay for the tea, but he made an offer to the British. He would pay for the tea if the tea tax was repealed. The British refused his offer. At the time of the Boston Tea Party, the tea was estimated to be worth 10,000 pounds in British currency. At today's value, that would be worth approximately $1.8 million!

A revision to the original 1765 Quartering Act went into effect as one of the Intolerable Acts in June 1774. Now, British soldiers could be housed in almost any building in the colony.

A fourth act, the Quebec Act, went into effect in June 1774. Britain did not consider it one of the Coercive Acts, but the colonists included it as an

Intolerable Act. Under the act, Canadian borders were extended to cut off the western parts of Connecticut, Massachusetts, and Virginia.

In reviewing the actions of the colonists, the British government also decided that Governor Hutchinson could not control the colony. He was replaced with a military governor, General Thomas Gage. The government also ordered that additional troops be sent to Massachusetts. Britain was determined to regain control of the colony.

THE COLONISTS RESPOND

Parliament's new laws did not silence talk of taxation without representation or diminish the concept of independence. The acts only increased the feelings of discontent in the Massachusetts colony. Discontent spread to the other colonies.

"Once vigorous measures appear to be the only means left of bringing the Americans to a due submission to the mother country, the colonies will submit."[1]

—*King George III*

When other colonies heard of the Boston Port Act, they decided to help Boston fight back. Maryland held its own tea party.

All of the other colonies began to send supplies to Boston. Rice, livestock, clothing, and even money were sent to the people of Boston so

Raspberry leaves were used for brewing tea.

they would have what they needed to survive. Never before had the colonies worked together so closely.

The idea of choosing drinks other than tea spread to other colonies. Brews made from raspberry leaves, herbs, fruits, and flowers replaced the traditional tea that came to the colonies via the East India

Company. This form of protest did not last very long, though. Habits are hard to break, and the taste of these drinks could be quite unappealing.

MILESTONE

The Massachusetts colony suggested reestablishing and strengthening nonimportation agreements. Though these agreements had been successful in the past, many colonies thought it was time for a stronger, more united resistance effort. At the suggestion of several colonies, Massachusetts agreed to a national congress to discuss the options available to the colonies.

All of the colonies, except Georgia, elected delegates to attend the First Continental Congress in September. This marked the first united attempt by the colonies to fight for their rights. ⁓

Labrador Tea

To protest the traditional tea from the East India Company, the colonists made Labrador tea from the herb Red Root Bush. The herb was plentiful and grew wild along the riverbanks of New England. American Indians were the first to make this tea, and they introduced it to the colonists.

Boston, Massachusetts, 1774

Carpenters' Hall in Philadelphia hosted the First Continental Congress.

The First Continental Congress

Delegates from 12 of the 13 colonies entered Philadelphia's Carpenters' Hall on September 5, 1774, to begin the First Continental Congress. Faced with problems of its own, Georgia had decided not to send a delegate. The Creek Indians were threatening its borders, and Georgia depended on British troops for protection. It did not want to risk losing that security should Britain decide to take revenge on those who participated in the Congress.

How could the delegates make Britain repeal the acts that had brought hardships to the colonies? Though the idea of independence may have made its way into the minds of some delegates, the First Continental Congress did not push the idea. There was still hope that a solution was possible without declaring and fighting for independence from British rule.

The Delegates

The delegates to the First Continental Congress were important people of the day. Future presidents included George Washington from Virginia and John Adams from Massachusetts. Samuel Adams was also among the Massachusetts delegates. Pennsylvania's delegates included the anonymous "Farmer"

Carpenters' Hall

Philadelphia's Carpenters' Hall hosted the First Continental Congress in 1774. It also served as home to Franklin's Library Company, The American Philosophical Society, and the First and Second Banks of the United States. The building has been owned since 1770 by the Carpenters' Company of the City and County of Philadelphia, the oldest trade guild in America.

John Dickinson. Patrick Henry represented Virginia.
John Jay, who would become the first chief justice of the
U.S. Supreme Court, was a delegate from New York.

Most of the delegates were from the upper classes and
involved in trade, farming, or law. These individuals
were respected in their communities, and it was
believed that their status could make the British
government take notice.

The First Continental Congress
convened in September 1774. Peyton
Randolph, a delegate from Virginia,
was selected to preside. He ran the
Congress from September 5 until
October 21. South Carolina delegate
Henry Middleton then was chosen
president of the Congress and ran
the proceedings from October 22
until its end on October 26.

First, the delegates considered a plan of union.
British loyalist Joseph Galloway of Pennsylvania
proposed that a united American council be formed.
Parliament and the council could veto each other's
actions when it came to matters dealing with America.
Galloway believed that if the colonies united, they
would have a stronger bargaining position.

Delegates were split on the issue. Had they not already negotiated enough? Could the colonies really act as one government, not as individual ones?

SUFFOLK RESOLVES

Before the Galloway proposal could be presented for a vote, Revere arrived with the Suffolk Resolves. This added more options to the discussion.

Representatives from Boston and other towns in Suffolk County, Massachusetts, had come up with a response to the Intolerable Acts. The Suffolk Resolves called for:

❖ The resignation of any official whose duty was to enforce the acts.

❖ Independence for Massachusetts until the Intolerable Acts were repealed.

❖ Taxes collected from the new Massachusetts to be kept by the government and not sent to Britain.

❖ A boycott of British goods and trade.

❖ The formation of a militia and arming of local forces in Massachusetts.

❖ The jailing of officers who arrested citizens for political reasons.

Citizen Committees

The citizen committees were effective. Because most of the communities elected the members, the citizen committees had the overwhelming support of the communities they served.

Also, subjects would not be loyal to a king who violated their rights.

Some delegates to the Congress thought passage of the Suffolk Resolves would lead to war. Others pushed for passage. The Suffolk Resolves were adopted, and Galloway's proposal for an American parliament was defeated.

Next, Congress considered adoption of the Continental Association, more commonly called the Association. If approved, this resolution would result in the following measures:

❖ The Association would ban all trade with Britain until Parliament repealed the Intolerable Acts.

❖ Citizen committees in each community would monitor and enforce the provisions of the act.

❖ Citizen committees would urge the public to be careful with using goods as the available supply would be greatly reduced.

The resolution calling for the establishment of the Association passed on October 20, 1774.

The First Continental Congress delegates also composed a letter to King George III stating their complaints. This Declaration of Rights and Grievances explained which parliamentary actions the colonies objected to and why. Both the colonists and the Sons of Liberty maintained their loyalty to the King. Their argument was with Parliament.

In this declaration, delegates stated that they should be considered equal to the British living in their homeland:

> *That our ancestors, who first settled these colonies, were ... entitled to all the rights, liberties, and immunities of free and natural born subjects within ... England.* [2]

Delegates believed the rights of their ancestors should pass down to their children and their children's children.

The declaration also asked for support from the British people:

> *To these grievous acts and measures Americans cannot submit, but in hopes that their fellow subjects in Great Britain will, on a revision of them, restore us to that state in which both countries found happiness and prosperity ...* [3]

George Washington is
called the Father of Our
Country. He probably
would not have agreed.

Peyton Randolph was
one of Washington's few
close friends. Randolph
was the president of the
First Continental Congress.
He taught Washington
much about politics.
When Washington learned
of Randolph's death, he
called Randolph the Father
of Our Country.

Not all of the delegates supported
the Declaration of Rights and
Grievances. Some believed it gave
too much power over trade to
Parliament. Nevertheless, the
document was approved and sent
to King George III.

Before the First Continental
Congress adjourned, delegates agreed
to meet in the spring of 1775 if the
King or Parliament had refused to
deal with the colonies' complaints.
With Second Continental Congress
scheduled (if needed), the meeting
adjourned. Most of the delegates
considered it a success—despite the
arguments.

Now, the real test would be how
King George III and Parliament
would respond. ⌒

This painting of General George Washington hangs in
Washington College's Custom House in Chestertown, Maryland.

Minutemen defending Bunker Hill, which overlooks Boston Harbor, 1775

AMERICA PREPARES TO FIGHT

*P*leased with what they had accomplished, delegates from the First Continental Congress returned to their colonies and waited for King George III and Parliament to respond. For the delegates and colonists living in the Boston area, there were clues that the response might not be favorable. The number of British soldiers increased, and the soldiers began gathering up the city's ammunition.

War appeared to be a certainty. Each colony established or strengthened its Committee of Safety. These committees were responsible for monitoring and acting on events that affected the public welfare. Each colony's committee was responsible for deciding when to send out the militia. The militia was made up of armed men prepared to defend their community from attack by foreign soldiers, in this case the British.

From within the militia, commanding officers selected a small group of men to serve as Minutemen. Minutemen had to be able to move into action quickly or "in a minute." They were usually the first ones on the scene of a battle. Though colonists had prepared for war, they still hoped for a peaceful solution.

Parliament gave its answer February 9, 1775. It declared the American colonies to be in a state of rebellion.

Who Were the Minutemen?

Minutemen were militia members, but not all members of the militia had what it took to be a member of the Minutemen. Members of the Minutemen were selected by commanders of the militia. Generally, they were under the age of 20 and younger than most of the militia. The young men were chosen because they had shown enthusiasm, strength, and determination. It was an honor to be selected.

LIBERTY OR DEATH

War seemed unavoidable. Colonists stepped up efforts to collect weapons and ammunitions. British troops stepped up their efforts to seize the colonists' weapons and ammunition. Additional British troops appeared in the colonies, especially in Massachusetts. Tension was higher than ever before.

The call went out for colonies to pledge troops for the war to come. Not all colonies favored participating in a military action. One of those colonies was Virginia. On March 23, 1775, Virginia's House of Burgesses debated the subject. Members were uncertain about their participation, especially since most of the conflict was in Massachusetts, far from the Virginia borders. The decision to send men to war was not an easy one, and the members of the House of Burgesses did not take their responsibility lightly.

THE VOICE OF LIBERTY

Patrick Henry's "Give me liberty or give me death" speech was not the only time he had roused the feelings of the members of the Virginia House of Burgesses.

This powerful speaker was born May 29, 1736, in Virginia. His speaking ability quickly became apparent in his law practice. In 1765, Henry was elected to the

*Patriot Patrick Henry was governor of Virginia
from 1776 to 1779 and from 1784 to 1786.*

Virginia House of Burgesses. In a May 1765 speech,
members of the House of Burgesses interrupted his
speech with calls of treason. They thought his speech
was suggesting the assassination of King George III.

Henry's participation in the fight for independence
was not limited to giving speeches. He also led a militia.

Though he supported independence, Henry was
very outspoken against the Constitution. He felt it

gave the federal government too much power. He was, however, a driving force in the adoption of the Bill of Rights, the first ten amendments to the Constitution.

Oddly, the words that led many to dub Henry the "Voice of Liberty" may never have been said. There are no copies of the "Treason" or "Give Me Liberty" speeches. What was said was left to people's memories, which may not always be accurate. It is likely he said something similar to those famous words, but perhaps not exactly those for which he is best known.

On March 23, 1775, Patrick Henry rose from his seat and addressed the Virginia House of Burgesses. He ended his speech with:

> Gentlemen may cry, Peace, Peace—but there is no peace. The war is actually begun! … I know not what course others may take; but as for me, give me liberty or give me death![1]

His words moved the members of the House of Burgesses. Some were so inspired they jumped up with cries of "To Arms!" while others cheered. The House agreed to commit troops to the conflict.

With troops committed, the American colonies were ready for the British.

RESTRAINING THE COLONIES

Though Parliament had called the American colonies rebellious, efforts were still underway to prevent war. Parliament spent much of the early part of 1775 debating how best to handle the colonies. Still trying to punish Massachusetts for the Boston Tea Party, they expected the colony to pay for the damage the Patriots had caused. So far, the colonists had not given any hint that they were sorry—or that any payment would be coming. Only boycotts and protests came from the colonists.

Some members of Parliament were willing to compromise with the colonies to avoid further conflict or war. The Earl of Chatham, a member of the British House of Lords, proposed that its government remove its troops from Boston. He hoped that if the British soldiers were removed from the source of most of the conflict, colonists might be more agreeable to the laws and taxes that Parliament had placed on them. His proposal was soundly defeated by the House of Lords.

But the Earl of Chatham was not ready to give up. He proposed that the colonies formally accept Parliament as the supreme governing authority and come up with their own plan for raising money. In return, Parliament would hold off on enforcing its tax acts and recognize the Continental Congress. Again the members of the House of Lords rejected his proposal.

The House of Lords was not alone in looking for a solution. Prime Minister Lord North was making his own proposal to the House of Commons. He proposed that the colonies take over the responsibility of taxing themselves. If they could raise enough in taxes to pay for their defense and the salaries of British officials stationed in the colonies, Parliament would not tax them. The proposal passed in the House of Commons. All that was left was passage by the House of Lords and King George III's signature.

What passed was the New England Restraining Act. On March 30, 1775, Parliament and the King added additional restrictions on the New England colonies:

❖ As of July 1, 1775, trade by New England to any country other than Britain and the British West Indies was prohibited.

❖ As of July 20, 1775, all of New England's ships were banned from North Atlantic fisheries.

This act would harm New England's economy, and Parliament was well aware of that.

To curb any ideas of resistance that might be brewing, the following month Parliament included Virginia, Pennsylvania, New Jersey, Maryland, and South Carolina under the act.

The colonists knew what was next.

War Begins

British troops had two goals for the early days of the conflict. They wanted to take the colonists' guns and ammunition. British troops were ordered to capture Adams and Hancock so the two could be sent to Britain to face charges of treason.

On April 18, 1775, approximately 700 British soldiers left Boston for Concord to destroy guns and ammunition. Patriot Joseph Warren learned of the plan. The town of Lexington was on the way to Concord. Warren knew Adams and Hancock were in Lexington. Warren called upon Paul Revere, William Dawes, and Samuel Prescott to warn Adams, Hancock, and the colonists in Concord. Revere knew the British troops were leaving Boston by water. He gave instructions for two lanterns to be hung in the steeple

The Old North Church

The Old North Church (officially Christ Church in the City of Boston) was built in 1723. It is the oldest standing church in Boston, and its steeple houses the oldest bells in North America.

At the time the church's steeple was used to signal Paul Revere of the oncoming British, most members of the church were Loyalist. Many of the members were officials of the British government.

of Boston's Old North Church to notify the Sons of Liberty in Charlestown. Adams and Hancock were warned and were gone by the time the troops arrived.

Instead of finding Adams and Hancock, British troops found 75 Minutemen—armed and ready. Though brave and enthusiastic, the Minutemen were outnumbered almost ten to one. Eight Minutemen were killed; another ten were wounded.

Revere was captured, but not until after he warned Adams and Hancock. Dawes made it to Concord and warned the citizens, who had time to move their guns and ammunition to other locations. When British soldiers arrived in Concord, they found and destroyed only a small portion of the town's weapons.

While soldiers searched for weapons, Minutemen from other towns responded to the warnings. They were joined by local farmers and residents. As British troops returned to Boston, they were attacked by the Minutemen and their supporters. By the time they reached their barracks, 73 British soldiers had been killed and many more were injured.

In less than two years, a protest in Boston Harbor that injured no one had evolved into full-fledged war. It was just the beginning of America's fight for independence. ⌒

Minutemen at Lexington Green, April 1775

TIMELINE

1763	1764	1765
Treaty of Paris is signed February 10, ending the French and Indian and Seven Years' Wars.	Sugar Act is passed April 5 to help pay for the recent wars.	Stamp Act is passed March 22.

1766	1767	1767
On March 18, the Declaratory Act is passed and the Stamp Act is repealed.	Townshend Acts are passed during June and July.	First segment of "Letters from a Pennsylvania Farmer" is published December 2.

1765

1765

1765

Quartering Act
is passed March 24.

Patrick Henry gives
his "Treason" speech
May 30.

Stamp Act Congress
opens in New York City
October 7.

1768

1770

1770

British troops
occupy Boston on
October 1.

Boston Massacre
occurs March 5.

On April 12,
Townshend Acts are
repealed, except for
the tax on tea.

TIMELINE

1772

1773

1773

The *Gaspee* incident
occurs June 9.

Tea Act goes
into effect May 10.

Boston Tea Party
occurs December 16.

1774

1774

1774

The Quartering Act
is revised June 2.

The Quebec Act
is passed June 22.

First Continental
Congress occurs in
Philadelphia September
22 to October 26.

1774

1774

1774

Benjamin Franklin
is called before the
Privy Council
January 29.

Boston Port Act
is passed March 31.

Massachusetts
Government Act and
Admin. of Justice Act
are passed May 20.

1775

1775

1775

Parliament declares the
colonies to be in
rebellion February 9.

Patrick Henry gives his
"Give Me Liberty"
speech March 23.

Battles of Lexington
and Concord occur
April 19.

ESSENTIAL FACTS

DATE OF EVENT

December 16, 1773

PLACE OF EVENT

Boston, Massachusetts

KEY PLAYERS

❖ Samuel Adams
❖ Paul Revere
❖ Thomas Hutchinson
❖ The Patriots
❖ The Sons of Liberty
❖ British Parliament

Highlights of Event

❖ Britain passed several acts to raise money to pay for the costs of wars and to maintain the colonies. Many colonists felt only the colonies had the right to tax their residents unless the colonies were represented in Parliament.

❖ Britain wanted to be paid for the tea ruined in the Boston Tea Party and the taxes it would have raised. The colonists continued to boycott British-taxed tea and cargo shipped by the East India Company.

❖ Parliament replaced the Massachusetts governor with a military governor and sent troops to help regain control of the colony. Other colonies supported Boston. This led to the formation of the First Continental Congress and the Declaration of Rights and Grievances. Parliament saw this as an act of rebellion. The War for American Independence was about to begin.

Quote

"The tree of liberty must be refreshed from time to time with the blood of patriots and tyrants."—Thomas Jefferson

ADDITIONAL RESOURCES

SELECT BIBLIOGRAPHY

An American Time Capsule: Three Centuries of Broadsides and Other Printed Ephemera. <http://memory.loc.gov>.

Bowdoin, James, Joseph Warren, and Samuel Pemberton. *A Short Narrative of the Horrid Massacre in Boston.* Williamstown, MA: Corner House Publishers, 1973. (Originally published 1770.)

Carr, Jacqueline Barbara. *After the Siege: A Social History of Boston, 1775–1800.* Boston: Northeastern University Press, 2004.

Galvin, John R. *Three Men of Boston.* New York: Thomas Crowell, 1976.

"Gaspee History." <http://www.gaspeeinfo.org>.

"The Harvard Guide: U.S. Presidents and Honorary Degrees." <http://www.hno.harvard.edu/guide/lore/index.html>.

Hewes, George. "Boston Tea Party: Eyewitness Account by a Participant." *America's Homepage.* Georgia Tech University. <http://ahp.gatech.edu/tea_party_account_1773.html>.

Labaree, Benjamin W. *Colonial Massachusetts: A History.* Millwood, NY: KTO Press, 1979.

Miller, Lillian B. "The Dye Is Now Cast." *The Road to American Independence, 1774–1776.* Washington, D.C.: The Smithsonian Institution, 1976.

FURTHER READING

Aronson, Marc. *The Real Revolution: The Global Story of American Independence.* Boston: Clarion Books, 2005.

Hossell, Karen Price. *The Boston Tea Party: Rebellion in the Colonies.* Portsmouth, NH: Heinemann, 2002.

Irvin, Benjamin H. *Samuel Adams: Son of Liberty, Father of Revolution.* New York: Oxford University Press, 2002.

Roza, Greg. *Analyzing the Boston Tea Party*. New York: Rosen, 2005.

Young, Alfred H. *The Shoemaker and the Tea Party: Memory and the American Revolution*. Boston: Beacon Press, 2000.

Web Links

To learn more about the Boston Tea Party, visit ABDO Publishing Company on the World Wide Web at **www.abdopublishing.com.** Web sites about the Boston Tea Party are featured on our Book Links page. These links are routinely monitored and updated to provide the most current information available.

Places to Visit

National Park Service Visitor Center
15 State Street, Boston, MA 02109
617-242-5642
www.nps.gov/bost/index.htm
This historic park includes sites such as the Paul Revere House, the Old South Meeting House, the Old North Church, and the site of the Boston Massacre.

Liberty Tree
Intersection of Washington Street and Essex Street, Boston, MA 02111
617-635-4505
www.celebrateboston.com/sites/libetytree.htm
The plaque on the building marks the spot of the famous tree used as a meeting place by the Sons of Liberty.

Old South Meeting House
310 Washington Street, Boston, MA 02108
617-482-6439
www.oldsouthmeetinghouse.org
Protest meetings that led to the Boston Tea Party were held here. Every December, a reenactment of the Boston Tea Party is presented. (Check the Web site for date and time.)

GLOSSARY

agenda
A formal list of things to be done and the order in which they are to be completed.

coercive
Having the power to make people do things against their will.

compromise
To settle a dispute by agreeing to accept less than what was wanted.

contraband
Goods that are illegally imported or exported.

dissent
Disagreement on a position.

duty
A tax on goods, especially imports and exports.

effigy
Dummy used to represent something disliked.

encampment
A campsite, especially one used for military purposes.

extremist
Someone who holds extreme or radical beliefs.

grievance
Complaint regarding the violation of a right.

House of Burgesses
Virginia's legislative body was the first form of representative government in the colonies.

House of Commons
The elected lower house of Parliament.

House of Lords
The non-elected upper house of Parliament.

imperial
Relating to the authority of one country over another.

intolerable
Unbearable.

Loyalist
An American who supported the British.

manslaughter
> The unlawful killing of a human being without intent to kill.

militia
> A group of citizens organized as soldiers.

negotiate
> To come to an agreement through discussion and compromise.

pamphlet
> A printed publication, often not bound.

Parliament
> The governmental body of Britain.

Patriot
> An American who supported the colonies.

prenuptial agreement
> Agreement made before a marriage.

prestigious
> Considered to be of high quality or a high honor.

Privy Council
> A group of advisers to the British monarch.

provision
> A clause in a contract or law stating that a particular condition must be met.

repeal
> To officially abolish.

revoke
> To formally cancel.

subordinate
> Lower in status.

unification
> The act of joining together.

vandalize
> To damage property or belongings.

veto
> The power of one branch of government to reject the legislation of another.

Source Notes

Chapter 1. The Most Famous Tea Party in History

1. George Hewes. "Boston Tea Party: Eyewitness Account by a Participant." *America's Homepage.* Georgia Tech University. 20 Nov. 2006 <http://ahp.gatech.edu/tea_party_account_1773.html>.

2. Ibid.

3. ThinkExist. "Samuel Adams." *ThinkExist.com Quotations.* 16 Nov. 2006 <http://thinkexist.com/quotes/samuel_adams/>.

Chapter 2. Challenging the Colonies

1. "Patrick Henry." *World of Quotes.* 16 Nov. 2006 <http://www.worldofquotes.com/author/Patrick-Henry/1/index.html>.

Chapter 3. Fanning the Flames

1. "Boston Non-Importation Agreement, August 1, 1768." <http://www.yale.edu/lawweb/avalon/amerrev/amerdocs/boston_non_importation_1768.htm>.

Chapter 4. The Sons (and Daughters) of Liberty

1. Robert Leckie. *George Washington's War.* New York: Harper Collins, 1990. 48.

2. ThinkExist. "Thomas Jefferson." *ThinkExist.com Quotations.* 16 Nov. 2006. http://thinkexist.com/search/searchquotation.asp?search=The+tree+of+liberty&q=author%3A%22Thomas+Jefferson%22>.

Chapter 5. Life in Boston

None.

Chapter 6. The Party

1. "Announcement of the Boston Tea Party." *Boston Gazette.* 20 Dec. 1773. Library of Congress. 4 Apr. 2007 <http://memory.loc.gov/learn/ features/timeline/amrev/rebelln/tea.html>.

Chapter 7. Important Participants

1. "Samuel Adams." *Liberty-Tree.ca.* 20 Nov. 2006 <http://quotes.liberty-tree.ca/quote/samuel_adams_quote_731a>.

2. ThinkExist. "John Hancock." *ThinkExist.com Quotations.* 16 Nov. 2006 <http://thinkexist.com/quotes/John_Hancock/>.

Chapter 8. After the Party

1. Franklin C. Baer, ed. "King George III." *Creative Quotations.* 16 Nov. 2006 <http://creativequotations.com/one/1013.htm>.

Chapter 9. The First Continental Congress

1. ThinkExist. "John Jay." *ThinkExist.com Quotations.* 16 Nov. 2006 http://thinkexist.com/quotation/those-who-own-the-country-ought-to-govern-it/533772.html>.

2. Steve Mount. "The Declaration of Rights and Grievances." *The U.S.*

Source Notes Continued

Constitution Online. 15 Mar. 2006. <http://www.usconstitution.net/ intol.html>.

3. Ibid.

Chapter 10. America Prepares to Fight

1. Patrick Henry. "Give Me Liberty or Give Me Death." *College of Law: A Chronology of Historical Documents.* 18 May 2006. The University of Oklahoma Law Center. 4 Apr. 2007 <http://www.law.ou.edu/ ushistory/henry.shtml>.

INDEX

Index Continued

ABOUT THE AUTHOR

Ida Walker is a freelance author and editor. A graduate of the University of Northern Iowa in Cedar Falls, she did graduate work at Syracuse University in New York. She is the author of several nonfiction books for middle-grade and young-adult readers on topics that include the United Nations, Ireland, illicit drugs, and Lynyrd Skynyrd and other music legends. She lives in upstate New York.

PHOTO CREDITS

North Wind Picture Archives: cover, title page, pp. 6, 13, 14, 23, 33, 34, 39, 43, 44, 51, 52, 59, 65, 69, 75, 77, 78, 86, 95
AP Images: pp. 24, 60, 70, 85, 89